KAYLA'S LONDON DAY OUT

BY ASHER AND
SIMON PROWER

THE KAYLA
ADVENTURES

About the authors:

Asher and Simon are a married couple and live in the South East of England. Asher was born in England, but is immensely proud of her Caribbean heritage....her roots being in St. Vincent and the Grenadines, where she visits regularly.

In Asher's words:

I was fortunate as my childhood and schooling was split between the UK and the Caribbean so I had the best of both worlds, and I gained a clear understanding of my Caribbean heritage from a young age. That made me the woman I am today and framed my passion for equality, diversity and inclusion.

Both as a child and an adult I have often been the only person of colour in a room. Representation is important and is key to us creating the character of Kayla.

"The Kayla Adventures" *will be a series of books where we aim to provide entertaining and educational reading books for all children regardless of skin colour, and gently introduce some of these themes.*

THE KAYLA ADVENTURES

Copyright © 2023 by Asher and Simon Prower
All rights reserved.
No part of this publication may be reproduced, distributed, or transmitted in any form or by any means, including photocopying, recording, or other electronic or mechanical methods, without prior written permission.

The story, all names, characters, and incidents portrayed in this production are fictitious, and all character illustrations are via AI software. No identification with actual persons (living or deceased), places, buildings, and products is intended or should be inferred.

Kayla and Emily are best friends.

They live in the same street and love playing together.

They go to the same school and often walk to school together, with their mummies or daddies.

Emily's mummy is planning a surprise!

"Emily and I are going to London tomorrow."

"Would you and mummy like to come with us?" she asked.

Kayla was very excited, especially when her mummy says yes!

Kayla wakes up very early the next morning.

She has breakfast then brushes her teeth.

Her daddy helps to brush her hair.

She rushes downstairs, looking out for Emily and her mummy.

Kayla and Emily talk while they wait for the train.

Their mummies also talk
...about boring
grown-up stuff!

"Look, here comes the train"
says Emily's mummy.

They play "I spy" on the train.

They see cows, horses, cars, lorries, and lots of bridges and tunnels.

The journey goes very quickly!

Kayla's mummy gives them a list of things to look for in London during the day!

A London Black Cab

A Red Telephone Box

A Double-Decker Bus

The London Eye

The Shard
(The tallest building in Europe!)

"I love visiting London" says Kayla, yawning.

Before the train has even left the station, Kayla is asleep!

At school a few days later, Emily and Kayla talk about their lovely London trip.

The trains, the museum, the dinosaurs, Big Ben, Tower Bridge.

It was so much fun!

Kayla especially loved the museum.

She has decided she definitely wants to be an adventurer when she grows up!

She is busy planning where to visit next....

THE END

Please look out for more stories from:
THE KAYLA ADVENTURES

As the train arrives in London, Kayla's mummy tells them that they are going to a museum.

The museum building is very large and old.

Kayla and Emily are amazed.....there are dinosaurs!

The dinosaurs aren't alive of course....but the skeletons and bones are fantastic!

Kayla can't believe the size of the T-Rex.

It's HUGE!!

She loves looking at the fossils.

Fossils are the remains of animals that lived a long time ago.

There are even real dinosaur teeth!

She sees lots of other large animals too.

The whale is enormous!

They also see lots of maps.

They learn how ships and explorers used to sail across the oceans.

After the museum, Kayla, Emily, and their mummies do lots of walking!

They see Buckingham Palace.

That's where the King lives.

The guards all look very smart in their uniforms.

They walk past Big Ben!

Kayla has seen it on television, but didn't realise how tall it is.

Kayla is tired! Emily is tired!

Both their mummies are tired!

They walk back to the station talking about the lovely day.

Kayla and Emily love playing the claw game.

Kayla wins a cuddly pink Elephant.

Emily wins a Teddy Bear.

They are both so happy.

It has been a long day and it is starting to get dark.

It is nearly time to go home.

They walk towards the railway station.

"One final treat" Emily's mum says.

"Would you like a quick game on one of those machines?"

Kayla and Emily enjoy crossing the river.

"It's called the River Thames" says Emily's mummy.

Kayla soon finds out what the surprise is!

They walk across Tower Bridge.

She has never seen a bridge like this before.

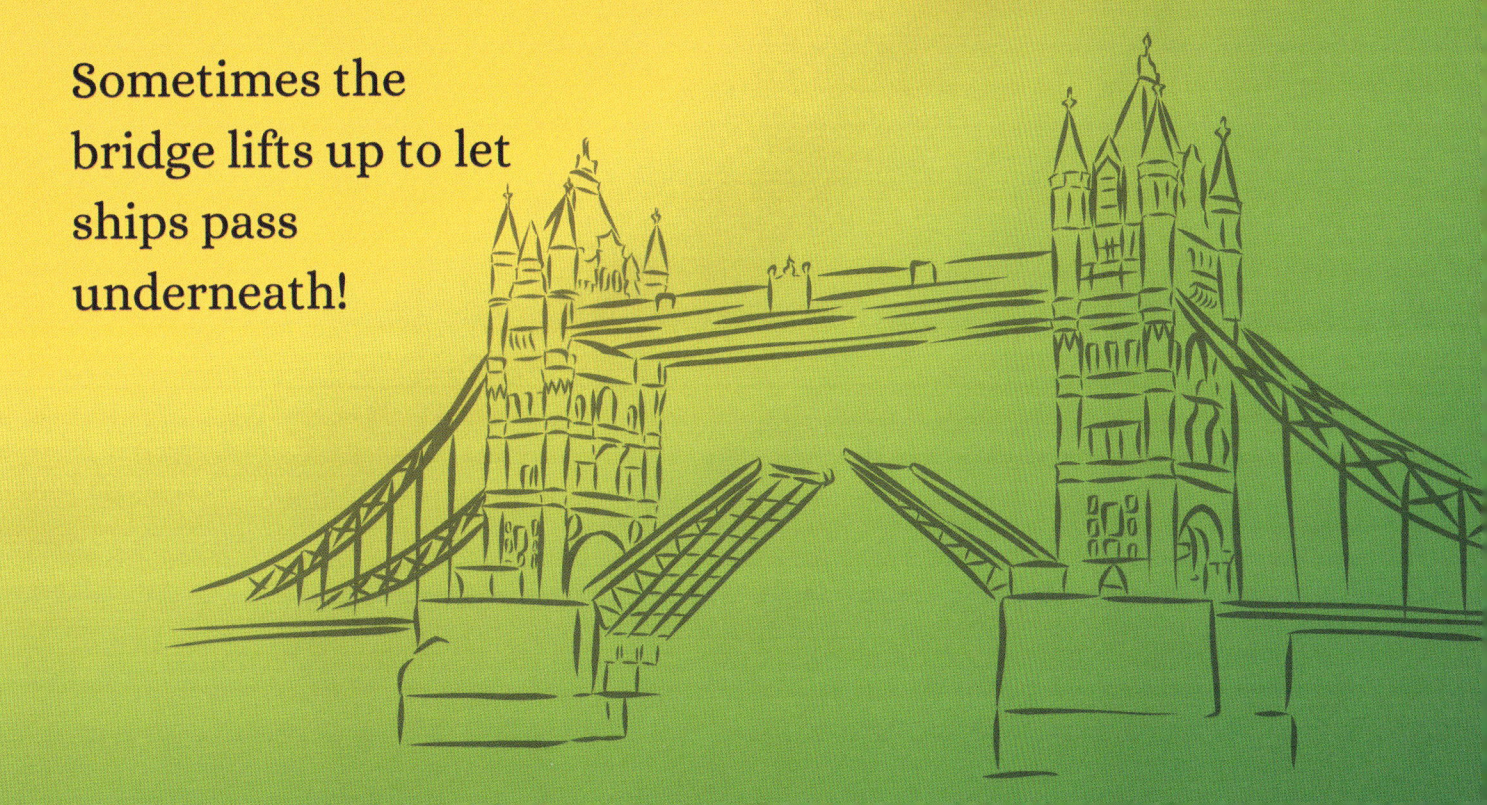

Sometimes the bridge lifts up to let ships pass underneath!

Emily's mummy won't tell them where they are going to next!

"It's a secret!" she says, smiling.

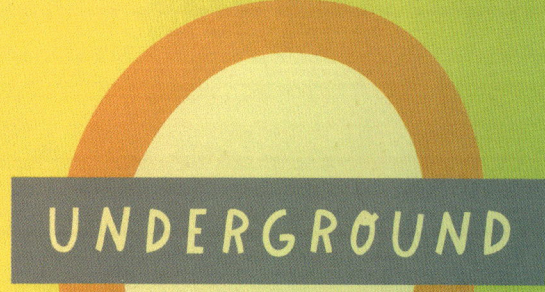

UNDERGROUND

Kayla is excited when they travel on an underground train....

....but she is very confused by the map!

This map has lots of lines, all different colours.

Kayla's mummy tells them that "Big Ben" is actually the name of the bell.

The bell is hidden behind the large clocks at the top of the tower.

Printed in Great Britain
by Amazon